The Aesthetic Market

MORE THAN MEETS THE EYE

BY

JOHN TREADWELL

ISBN-10: 0982773722

ISBN-13: 978-0982773727

Perfected Pen Publishing
www.PerfectedPen.com
www.SabrinaKCarpenter.com
www.PerfectedPenPublishing.com

Dedication

This Fabulous book is dedicated to:

Joseph Mark Buice, whose support, love and dedication is beyond priceless.

My adoring cat, Valentino, who stayed by my side throughout this entire project.

Rosaline Odell Alexander Treadwell, who is my true definition of Fabulous.

Be Yourself

What I have heard all of my life is that I need to change. I need to change the way I dress, I need to change the way I say things – told that it is not what I say but how I say it. I have heard that all of my life. Some of the most famous people we recognize, are known for their strong personalities and are not always pleasant. If these people had listened to others and changed and became more mainstream, would they have been as successful? I think this strength of personality is a positive contribution to their (and my) success. Trying to implement the steps to bring positive change to a practice has been met with resistance since the day I started. I heard so many excuses. "We cannot do this in our community, town, city, state, office..." and on goes the list of places that it cannot be done. If I had listened to the excuses, this book would not exist. If I had listened, the success that exists throughout the country within the aesthetic market would not be in place and would not be creating additional revenue for physicians throughout the country. If I had listened, I would not have taken my current path in life. Coming from a family that valued beauty but not as a career, I would have chosen the traditional accountant's life or minister's life. Be proud of going against the crowd. Be your own person. Always be yourself!

"The razor was looked upon as a joke by all my friends. A common greeting was, 'Well, Gillette, how's the razor?' If I had been technically trained, I would have quit."

King Gillette, Gillette Razors

My Journey

After 30 years in the beauty business, at the age of 50, I decided to retire. I had a lifetime of memories working with some of the best in Hollywood. I had fond memories with the best companies and employment opportunities that anyone could ever ask for. Being very competitive and driven, I always wanted to win any contest the companies would bring my way because the challenge was exciting for me. I was consistent and won every contest prize that was available. My drive to win and ability to think outside of the box, consistently paid off. While others were trying to invent new and different ways of winning, I simply went back to what always worked for me; old fashioned marketing.

I would partner with those in the community and reward those that made me successful. Most importantly, I would thank the customers that made me accomplished. At first, it was the only thing I knew but I secretly thought that there must be a better way so I purchased books to learn new and different ways to market and build businesses. After all, you're never too old to learn new tricks.

After years of successful work experience, upon retirement I looked back and had that relatable feeling of, "If I had known starting my work career what I know now, I could have saved myself many sleepless nights and much aguish!" But, life is a learning process.

I enjoyed doing crafts during my retirement along with what most others do; going out to lunch, traveling, watching TV, walking and of course reading. But, the real task I wanted to accomplish was to write a book. I needed to put my experiences into book form and help those trying to accomplish some of the same feats without trying to reinvent the wheel. Typically, all of the work has been done before us and does not need much tweaking. It's just a matter of gaining access to the results-driven information.

About 6 years into retirement, life got in the way. By life, I really mean cancer got in the way. Just when I thought I had beat all of life's tragedies, "life" gets in the way, once again. It was highly frustrating.

My reality became three months of radiation therapy along with the wakeup call that I was not invincible. Tired, depressed and feeling vulnerable, I decided to move to Key West. I had always wanted to live there and it was also one of the things on my bucket list.

After completion of radiation, I decided to get the bucket list out and start checking things off. I realized I might not have the amount of time to fulfill these goals as I originally expected. Upon my retirement, I started riding motorcycles and it was my goal to ride my bike across the Seven Mile Bridge. I was able to quickly check two things off; moving to Key West and riding my motorcycle across the Seven Mile Bridge. But, I still had too much time on my hands and it was becoming an enemy.

I needed to go back to work to occupy my mind, work my worn-out body and nourish my soul. I was tired of learning life lessons the hard way and really just needed to escape myself.

I decided to do skincare in an office that did injectables and toxins. The main reason was because I was now of a certain age that could (and should) use fillers and toxins. I thought if I worked in an office with them and actively promoted their services, maybe I could get a little something as a bonus. As it turns out, I certainly was rewarded by them and was completely hooked after the first filler and wrinkle smoother. I also learned I could use the same back-to-basic techniques for marketing that I had used for my own career.

I didn't realize at the time, but I was reinventing myself once again. I mainly looked at it as busy work to keep my mind off of my health issues until the point came when I was comfortable that I had won the battle against cancer. Little did I know how addicted to fillers I would become and how much I actually enjoyed the industry. I utilized my marketing skills from 40 years of experience and made a difference in people's lives in a number of Fabulous ways.

After living in Key West and checking off items on my bucket list for two years, I decided it was time to move to the mainland. I always said if I ever lived near the ocean, I would never leave. I had an ex just a few hours north of Key West who was familiar with the city and I decided that would be the place to retire, yet again. I never understood why old people moved to Florida until I became one.

Settled in the house my ex owned, I ordered my Lazy Boy recliner and was ready to enjoy retirement (again). But, the doctor I went to in my town did fillers and toxins and wanted to expand his Aesthetic practice. He asked if I would help build the practice for no actual salary but instead, a percentage of profit. I asked what kind of budget I had to decorate the treatment room with and what kind of budget I had to promote the business. He quickly said zero. No longer young and adventurous but old and confident, I said yes. Pulling from that 40 years of basic marketing that had proven successful time and time again, I began the journey.

And what follows is what I leave as my legacy of life; Concierge Service in the Aesthetic Market. When implemented correctly, it should bring you much success and fulfillment, as it has for me.

"I never dreamed about success. I worked for it."

Estee Lauder

Starting a Concierge Aesthetic Practice

If a practice has no, or few, patients and wants to start a Concierge Aesthetic Practice as a stand-alone practice or incorporate it into a current practice in order to expand the practice and increase the revenue, below are proven recommendations for a cost-efficient and service-oriented Concierge Aesthetic Practice. The staff should be recruited and properly trained in the importance of Concierge Service within the Aesthetic Practice to ensure the highest level of success. Keep in mind, this is merely a checklist as a guideline…be sure to read all the way through the book for a full array of steps to implement for the ultimate success!

1. Experienced, licensed injector – if not a physician, a medical director is needed.
2. A practice concierge – consultations, events, one phone number contact, orders products and supplies. One phone number should be dedicated to all toxins and fillers and

be transferable to the concierge's cell phone for true Concierge Service 24/7. This sets the practice apart from everyone in town.

3. A Fabulous Face of the practice located up-front, greeting the patients and having paperwork completed – call and confirm appointments, call patients for follow-up, can also double as the accountant in the beginning and if funds are limited, they can also do payroll, etc. Add people as the business grows. (every $500,000 - add a person)
4. A minimum of two aesthetic rooms are necessary. One room for injections and the second room to do a consultation so the injector can go from room-to-room without delay.
5. A small room for standardized photography of every patient is useful but can be done in the injection room, if necessary, to cut expenses.
6. The concierge needs a private office to schedule and check people out in a calm and private setting.
7. Other aesthetic rooms are beneficial for aesthetician and/or renting the room to aestheticians – Fabulous source for referrals!

An important part of this plan is to hold a number of events outside of the practice and maintain the one voice of the practice inside the practice.

The Voice of the Practice

When I came to a particular practice, I saw things both inside and outside of the building that needed to be changed immediately. After a few days of observation, I noted that the phones were being answered by several people. I knew this was the first place to begin positive change for the Aesthetic Practice to blossom into a Concierge Practice.

I wanted all calls for fillers and toxins to come into one number answered by only one person. I chose a number preciously used as a rollover number and dedicated that line for Aesthetics only. I had the number transfer the call to an iPhone so that all filler and toxin phone calls can be answered 24/7. All brochures and business cards, including the doctor's and website content need to reflect this number. Realistically, the phone will not actually be answered at two in the morning, but if a voice message was left, the return phone call could be made in a timely manner the next morning.

The Concierge model set the practice apart from all of the other aesthetic practices in town. Being available by phone gives you the ability to put concerned patients at rest so the issue does not grow in their mind. To answer a call Saturday morning about a procedure you did Friday afternoon can be a huge asset for a concerned patient. It can eliminate the panic call or visit Monday morning by calming concern about swelling and bruising.

Answering a call at an unexpected time usually gets an amazed response of, "I thought I would get an answering machine!" The feeling instilled for the patient is that someone genuinely cares at this office and they ultimately feel special.

One person answers all calls and develops that medical relationship with the patients. The patient knows who will be answering and that can be comforting for them. One other person should also answer all incoming calls from new patients. When a new patient calls with questions, you can determine how long the appointment should be.

- Has the patient had any surgical work, previous fillers and/or toxins?
- How old is the patient?
- What are the patient's issues that they want to correct?

- What is their budget?
- How did they hear about your practice?

This information is very important to determine how effective your marketing has been. If the patient is a referral, it is important to say thank you to the referring source.

A determination has to be made through this "mini" phone consultation whether this is going to be 15-minute visit for a low-cost toxin or if this is a person who requires more.

A 30-45 minute appointment could be more appropriate for the patient wanting fillers and toxins. Since one person will be taking all of the aesthetic calls, that person makes the appointments. Utilizing the knowledge of the patients, the ability to schedule placement of the new or returning patient on a busy, packed schedule, is enhanced. This knowledge also allows them to be more in touch with cancelations and the flexibility to make quick changes in the schedule for replacements, preventing a day from disintegrating profit.

Being realistic, there are times when an incoming call simply cannot be taken. However, the return of the call and message should be a priority. As soon as the situation that prevented you from taking the call is complete, call the patient, express concern and apologize for not being available to take the incoming call. The phone is the first contact for most potential new patients and the method most returning patients use to secure the perfect appointment.

The person having the responsibility of the "voice" of the practice should have a voice that is easily understood with impeccable manners. The only thing that sets your practice apart from all of the other practices, is this level of service.

The patient very likely drives by other locations for the same services. The voice of the practice should give the calling patient a "call to action" like extending an invitation for them to come in to talk about the possibilities at absolutely no charge. Your potential new patient should not have their first impression be that you are "nickel and diming" them.

If the patient hears in the consultation what they want to hear, the services will be the same day as the consult. The person answering the phone with a cell phone can take that call anywhere; at the mall or on a weekend getaway. This one change to the practice starts the change to Concierge Service, which leads to growth. It is difficult to say what one single change made the most difference but this change is definitely up there with the best changes made for revenue increase.

Don't be afraid to mystery shop your practice. Have someone call with a set of questions and see how the person answering the call rates. Also, have someone do the same call but as a consultation. The answers will give you valuable tools for training and valuable tools for rewarding Fabulous service.

It is important that the voice of the practice conveys to every patient that you have a 100% guarantee policy for all of your products and services. I have a policy that all skin care is a "bottom of the bottle" guarantee with a full refund if they do not like the product. I believe a patient cannot tell after a few uses if the product is working and cannot tell if they like the product at that point. I want the patient to use the entire contents before deciding whether or not to return it.

This one addition has helped to reduce returns and has created more satisfied patients. This guarantee also should cover all services. It is better to take the high road and do additional services at no cost in order to create goodwill in the community. This is a benefit you cannot purchase, but must earn. Including skin care in the cost of a package of services is a Fabulous way to not only have better results for the service but also introduce even the most reluctant patient to your skin care products, creating future sales when they see the Fabulous results.

It is very important to find out why the patient left their last practice. This information can benefit you and provide you with the tools to ensure you are able to retain them rather than have them move on from you as they did the last. It is much less expensive to retain a patient than try to attract a new patient. Be sure and send a goodie bag home with all new patients. It can include a nail file with the practice information, an herbal tea bag and a sample of your skin care line. Be sure to include two business cards; one for home and one for the purse.

Create a receipt envelope. The envelope with the practice branding information can contain the receipt for services, the card with their next appointment, any coupons for services along with some beauty tips as an added bonus. Set yourself apart from the competition. Concierge Service in the aesthetic market may be what makes your patient want to tell someone about you and recommend that they visit you, as well. Always ask your patient about their experiences. Remember, an appointment ends but an experience continues.

The voice of the practice can also help create new brand recognition. News shows air seven days a week and are always looking for segments to fill space and feature local happenings. Be sure to send press releases for new products and services. Local talk radio also seeks regular features 24 hours a day, so be sure to send the stations your press releases for products and services, as well.

Staying open at least one late night each week and one Saturday a month to accommodate our patients' busy lives can increase revenue. I review the schedule for the injector several weeks in advance to monitor the need to add evening or extended hours and weekends. Set yourself apart from what everyone else is doing in town and accommodate the patient. They will reward you with many referrals and return visits.

"Long-term success is never achieved on our own. The phrase 'a self-made man' is a myth – all along the way we need support."

Issy Sharp, Four Seasons Hotels

The Face of the Practice

The voice and the face can be the same person creating the ultimate of Concierge Service. One person offering contact over the phone and in person gives the patient a feeling of safety.

Getting the doctor out of his or her own way is what we are about to tackle. Doctors are taught early on to be in control, and for most doctors, control is difficult to relinquish.

- Doctors should not give the initial consultation.
- Doctors should not know the price of anything.
- Doctors should not schedule, answer the phone or greet the patients.

Set the doctor apart and use the doctor's talents to produce revenue. While a consultation is being conducted, a doctor should be injecting the previous consultation, making the most efficient use of talent and time. The doctor does not make money by talking, only injecting. This adjustment is another on the list of the most important changes made in the practice for increased revenue.

The face of the practice greets all new and returning patients. Open the door and announce the name that you are ready for. When the patient rises, find something Fabulous about them to comment on.

"Your hair look great!"

"Those shoes are wonderful!"

"What a beautiful smile!"

...anything positive to put them at ease. Remember, the new patient has just completed paperwork and is waiting to be reminded of their flaws and then may have needles injected into their face. The returning patient is waiting for the review of previous visits and the possibility of additional needles in their face.

Both new and returning patients need to be in a relaxed state for the most effective visit to occur. While walking to the room, it is important to get a smile to soften the tension. Their shoulders are typically under their ears in tension. The statement I have found to be most effective is, "Let's go to the Beauty

Buffet, where everything is possible…only limited by your imagination…and I have a vivid imagination!"

Before the treatment begins, pictures should be taken in a controlled manner. A series of 7 pictures with eyes open and the same series with eyes closed should be taken for medical records and picture books with a signed release by the patient. The same series of pictures should be taken immediately after the procedure.

Most patients do not want their picture taken, so it is important to relax them and prevent objections. The statement that often works well is, "Let's go to the Olan Mills studio on Sunset Boulevard…you are ready for your close-up!" It lightens the mood and allows the client to feel assured.The face of the practice also completes the initial consultation to be able to provide the doctor with the needed information, as well as take care of the financials. A consultation should always be direct and truthful.

A consultation should talk about the "elephant in the room". There is a reason the patient made an appointment and it should be addressed. I believe you can teach anyone to do consultations if they are willing to be direct. Every consultation should start with information gathering.

What does the patient see as their strongest concern?

Many will volunteer the information that their husband does not want them to spend the money or that their spouse insists they look good the way they are. Their mothers tell them they look fine, too and that it would be ridiculous to change anything.

I tell the patient that both their husband and mother need glasses. The truth is that the husband does not want her to spend money and mothers will always love her children just as they are. The patient would not have made the appointment if what they were told, was actually true.

The consultation is also about information gathering. How old are they? Have they had facial surgery before? Have they had fillers and if so, how did they like the results?

Most filler patients coming in for a consultation, are the 40 and above patients, except for those wanting lip augmentation. At ages over 40, the patient has not only collagen loss but bone loss, as well. Fillers are ideal for the replacement of both.

A facelift does not negate the need for fillers. In fact, it actually emphasizes the need. Most patients after investing in a Liquid Face Lift, decide not to go the scalpel route.

The nasal labial folds are more prominent nearest the nose, softening as they reach the mouth. This bone loss, collagen loss and the face falling down and forward, gives the person doing the consultation an enormous amount of fodder for their use.

The chin becomes more prominent with this bone and collagen loss. The chin takes on what I say in the consultation is a "witchy" chin that they did not have in pictures from 10, 15, or 20 years prior. This patient also is experiencing loss in the cheeks which many times creates a malar crease.

Their cheek that once sat so high and proud is now resting just above the nasal labial folds helping to create a more pronounced fold. This patient is likely also experiencing under eye bags and pronounced tear troths.

The other side of this under eye issue is the patient that has had under eye surgery. Most eye lifts leave the under eye with lack of volume, creating a hollowing and shadowing effect. The upper lids many times are tightened and hallowed as well, needing filler.

The temple experiences significant loss and gives the most dramatic improvement when used to do the liquid facelift. It simulates the traditional facelift by emulating the upward motion and replacing the volume loss.

Jaw line augmentation can also help soften the marionette lines or what I like to refer to as the "bull dog" jowls. Filler is needed above the brow bone to lift the outside corners of the brow and filler in a u-shape around the forehead to lift the brows are also possible.

The possibilities are endless for fillers and quantity is needed to have transformational work. Most patients in their 40s need a minimum first treatment of 8 syringes. In their 50s, they should begin with 12 syringes, and then add 4 syringes for each decade after.

For the 8 syringe treatment, 2 syringes each are used in the temples, under the eyes and cheeks, nasal labial folds and to soften each side of the chin. Pointing this out to the patient with a mirror shows the need for a significant amount of filler and not the one or two they thought were needed.

I refuse to do the one or two syringe treatment. I state we do not do small numbers as it is like putting a cup of water in a bathtub full of water…it will not get noticed. The client just wouldn't be happy and tomorrow they will very likely have buyer's regret for spending money and not seeing results.

The patient would be correct that they don't see correction because not enough product was used. This disappointed patient will be a pain in the practice for the rest of their life. They will never be happy and will want more for no cost.

Even though I say that the practice will not do 1 or 2 syringe treatments, I have never lost a patient from this. It is the reality check that some people need. Do not be afraid of large volume treatment! The large volume patient will send you referrals and be your happiest patient because you have done truly transformational work.

The question of cost should be addressed head on in the consultation. Inform the patient of the cost and quietly wait for their response. The most common response is that they can't afford it. When that occurs, I do not say a word in response. I simply get up and get a "care credit" application on a clipboard with a pen. I tell them (don't ask!) to fill out the form and I will get the account opened before the consultation is complete. Truthfully, I don't really care about the application, I just want to call their bluff.

Most respond that they will pay by check or use their credit card and then you have gotten them to commit to the procedure. Keep in mind, some will continue to say they cannot afford the procedure. I do not acknowledge a "no" response until the third time it is said.

The second time I hear the "no" response I ask them, "If it were you mother, daughter or sister, and they felt strongly about wanting to make these kind of improvements, would you help them?" Many times that triggers a "yes" response and allows them to realize that they deserve the procedure, also.

There are times that you will get the response that they can put "x" amount of dollars on their credit card. Either way, you will begin to know what they can truly spend.

For the person who says they can afford only 4 syringes, my response is, "Let's make your face our project!" I always want the person to know that with only 4 syringes we will not be doing a liquid facelift and will only be softening the look.

With fewer syringes, it is important to target one specific area rather than spreading it around the entire face and seeing little results. It is far better to see results in one area. I advise them that we will start with the 4 syringes today and at their future appointments we will add additional syringes as their budget allows.

Always be forthcoming when talking about where you are going to use the 4 syringes, rather than the 8 recommended. It is best to always go up. Start with the temples and cheeks and it will in turn help the lower face, as well.

Chase the solution not the problem! Filling the nasal labial fold, as most people request, creates a primate look if the bottom of the face becomes over-filled. When patients continue to fill the bottom half of their face and ignore the top half, they start to look like Mama was a duck and Daddy was a monkey. Everything is falling on the face so do not put more where it has already fallen.

Confirm the price and placement. Excusing yourself, tell the patient you are going to get the doctor. Put a video on about the practice or about the fillers you discussed for the patient to watch or give them brochures about the products and leave before and after photo books.

Do not have any magazines or newspapers in the room, as you want them to read only information about your services. A magazine with pictures of stars with facial work gone wrong is not what you want your aesthetic patients looking at and reading about while waiting.

When you approach the doctor, you are now armed with information valuable to the doctor. For example, we have Jane Doe, new patient referred by Mary Smith. Jane is 63 years old and had a facelift 9 years ago. 8 months ago she had filler and toxin and her concern is volume loss in her cheeks and nasal labial folds. She has agreed to do 7 syringes today and 40 units of toxin.

Now, the doctor goes in prepared and does not have to worry about discussing money. The doctor should NEVER discuss money with the patient, only the procedure. If the doctor decides to do 6 syringes and 35 units of toxin today, the patient is pleased as the cost has just been reduced and the patient is happy.

The doctor is always the one to decide what the procedure will entail and the initial consultation is for information gathering, information sharing and getting the cost out of the way so the doctor does not have to discuss any financials.

If the doctor is confronted with the cost question, they should politely excuse themselves saying they need to check a quick voicemail and leave the room allowing the Face of the practice to discuss any financial inquiries. Once the issues have been addressed, the doctor can return moments later to complete the procedure.

While the doctor is handling the procedure, the Face of the practice is doing the consultation for the next patient. The doctor should leave the room as soon as the last syringe is empty. When the doctor comes out, the Face of the practice informs the doctor of the next patient and the important information needed before going into the next room.

The process continues in harmony with everyone doing what they do best. It is the most efficient way to build a profitable practice. I like to go in when I think the doctor is on the last syringe and tell the patient they are looking great. I then suggest they are only a couple of syringes away from being truly Fabulous. This is a way to add the extra syringes needed at the end to increase profits and results. This added step is quite effective most of the time. Who would want to leave less than Fabulous?

Every patient should return for a no-cost follow up face check-up in 10 days to 2 weeks after their procedure. Every patient should also leave with a skincare regime. A minimum of cleanser, eye crème and moisturizer is the perfect starter. Always do the series of before and after photos at every visit. We always want to tweak to perfection.

When they return, they are happy and hooked on fillers. At the return visit consultation, the patient reveals their pleasure and or concerns. This is the time to address concerns and suggest additional filler to enhance the results.

You always want to focus on balance. One nasal labial fold may be fuller than the other. Tweaking with a small amount of filler also gets the needle in the face, opening the door for more filler purchases. It also demonstrates to the patient that you genuinely care about their appearance.

You now have the information needed to inform the doctor before they go in for the follow up visit. Once again the doctor knows no pricing and leaves after treatment. After the procedure "after" photos are taken and another complimentary follow-up visit is scheduled to tweak to Fabulous, you continue the cycle of the patient returning and their need for more product.

A returning patient of long standing is returning for purposes similar to the new patient. There is something that they want to address and a consultation solves the mystery. It may have been a year since their last visit and they need more product or they may want to address other areas on their face since they like the results of work done previously.

Everyone needs a consultation at every visit, whether it's a brief question or a complete interview. Do not pass up this valuable opportunity to point out the needs the patient has to purchase additional product.

A consultation should also include discussion on other services. Laser, radio frequency and whatever other services your practice offers. Combination therapy of multiple modalities with fillers and toxins produce the happiest patient with the most remarkable results. This Fabulous "before and after" result can be included in your picture books as long as the patient signs a release.

Always ask for the release!

Some will agree to it if you crop the photo. If there are remarkable results, this patient request would be worth the effort. Books by category in the consultation room are important. Categories could include lips, cheeks, nasal labial folds and/ or by product brand name.

It is important to inform the patient of the quantity of product needed. Most patients do not realize the amount needed, so at every opportunity remind the patient that quantity is needed for quality. I think it's very important to never leave the patient alone for an extended period of time. Someone in the room to keep the conversation going will go a long way in preventing the patient from changing their mind. Keep them talking about themselves, everybody wants to be heard and they will leave feeling as if the practice cares.

One more thing about the consultation…I think it is important to be truthful with the patient about their treatment plan. Just because you are doing 10 syringes today does not mean you are complete and that the patient will never need more. You may do 10 syringes today and in a few months do 5 more syringes and then in a few more months do an additional 3 to get to the desired liquid facelift results.

I always want to keep the patient informed so I can offer them truthful information, as well as a call to action to purchase more product today.

I think tiered pricing is a valuable tool to create a reason to purchase today. Tiered pricing allows you to create a call to action at checkout for the entire treatment plan. At checkout, I price the first syringe at $1000 (as an example) and all additional syringes used that day are $900. If the patient purchases the treatment plan at checkout for syringes that they are not using today, they are allowed to purchase at $800/syringe for today, and today only.

If the patient says, "No, I will just wait and pay when I come back in," I will inform them that I will be marking in their chart that they have chosen to pay $1000 when they come back in, rather than the $800 I offered today.

At least half of patients will then understand the savings that is being offered and decide to pre-purchase the treatment plan outlined in the consultation. Creating this call to action is important in any sales position and is no different in the aesthetic market. Give your patient a reason to purchase today and save money and they generally will.

This same call to action is effective during events. An event traditionally is about 3 hours and for that limited time, purchases can be made at the event for reduced prices, but only during this limited time. Create a reason to spend money and spend it now. No matter what echelon the patient belongs, they all like a deal or reason to buy now at a discounted price. I have found the ones with the most money actually like it the most and have the most money to spend at whim for the call to action. Many of your working folks would like to spend today but have budget restraints. Still plant the seed because at a future event they could be one of your best purchasers of pre-sales.

As the voice of the practice, always attend networking events. It could be a chamber of commerce breakfast monthly or their monthly business after hours. Most cities have multiple opportunities to network and most allow for at least a short commercial for participating.

"We must motivate ourselves to do our very best, and by our example lead others to do their best as well."

S. Truett Cathy, Chick-fil-A

The Hand of the Practice

Hand-written and hand-addressed correspondence is a lost art. No email thank you or form letter should ever be sent. No address labels should ever be used in the practice, for any purpose. Every new patient should receive a hand-written, hand-addressed thank you note. Every person attending an event of yours should receive a hand-written, hand-addressed thank you note. All notes should include business cards, as well as a call to action. I cannot stress this enough!

A call to action can include a business card inviting them to bring a friend with them at their next visit and both will receive $100 off their purchases of filler. Hand-written thank you notes have received more compliments than any single service we provide. Hand-written, hand-addressed notes will set you apart from the rest.

Once a quarter, send postcards for the season. On each hand-addressed card, write a line about all of the fillers and toxins that are on sale and for them to call for details. This is another call to action that creates excitement and additional revenue.

Every patient has a birthday and should receive a birthday card with a Fabulous offer from your practice. Reasons to send patients hand-written notes with a call to action are only limited by your own imagination. Anniversaries, Valentine's Day, Spring, Summer, Fall, Holidays, New Year, "thanks for being a loyal patient", "thanks for the referrals", etc. You get the point. Take advantage of these stellar opportunities to get patients in your door.

The attention to detail with the personalized notes should not stop there. Ensure you have refreshing beverages to offer everyone. A pitcher of cucumber and/or lemon water is a touch that easily sets you apart. Herbal teas are welcomed by many and are easy to keep in stock.

Ice packs with the practice information imprinted on them for patients to take home, is another touch that keeps your contact information readily available. Most people keep this ice pack in the freezer for future use and the contact information is always easily accessible.

Another touch that receives favorable response is checking people out after treatment in the comfort of the office with the

Voice of the practice. A credit card machine on the desk along with the computer is all that is needed. The patient is more comfortable not being in the general population after treatment, as most are concerned about their appearance without makeup.

A gift bag is another nice unexpected touch. It could include brochures and information of additional services you offer with a call to action offer upon their return. Also include a sample of a product you sell and a small mirror for their purse with the practice information. Do not forget to write the hand-written, hand-addressed thank you note after they leave. Also, do not forget to add their email address to you Constant Contact list so you can send an easy invitation to your events.

Referrals are the best new patients possible. A referral is usually the easiest patient in which to do a consultation. They came because a doctor recommended your practice or someone they know had procedures and look Fabulous.

All referrals should be rewarded!

I want to send something from outside the practice. I find if I send them a practice related thank you gift that it feels as if strings are attached. "Come spend more money with the practice and we will give you something."

If you send a gift certificate to a local restaurant, it is a genuine gift, no strings attached. Go to local restaurants and ask if they would like you to send your patients and referring doctors gift certificates to their restaurant and you will get a resounding, "Yes!"

Ask the owner to sell you $100 gift certificates for $50 and they will likely do so with pleasure. Don't be surprised if other restaurants start to contact you, asking if you will utilize their establishment and may offer even better cost savings. Some may even start to provide gift certificates at no cost.

Another way is to barter with restaurants for the gift certificates. Same principle, just a different approach and both approaches work effectively.

Use your gift certificates to reward other doctors who send you patients.

Use your gift certificates to reward patients who send friends, neighbors and relatives.

Use your gift certificates to reward hairdressers and aestheticians who send you patients.

Referrals are the best new patients, so reward those that send you the best. You will be surprised how many more they send you if you send them a genuine gift with no strings attached and with no reason to spend more money with you. Always send the thank you gift certificate with a hand-written and hand-addressed note of thanks.

If someone sends you three people in one day send them three separate gift certificates in three separate hand-written notes and hand-addressed envelopes. You will be surprised how many meals you provide in your community and how some people like it so much that they start sending you more referrals and never pay for dinner again.

Another important way to develop a referral business is to pair with local hairdressers and aestheticians to get filler in their face. I have a proposal stating that if you send me a new patient that purchases 4 syringes of filler, I will give 1 syringe for your use.

Remember, I will not do 1 syringe of filler, so they need to send me more clients to accumulate enough filler for a transformational result. Part of the agreement states that they must call and make the appointment for their client while their client is in their chair. It is a direct call to action to receive the reward of free filler. It is concierge service for the patient. If the hairdresser gives their client a business card with my name on it and tells them to call when they get home to make an appointment, it does not count. They must call while the client is in their chair. I keep the reward program on a spreadsheet to insure accuracy.

"Everybody likes something extra, for nothing."

William Wrigley Jr., Wrigley Chewing Gum

Dress the Face of the Practice

Everyone on the team, including the doctor, should wear clean, ironed, embroidered, white lab coats. This touch shows consistency and easily identifies who is on the team. The coat should have the name of the practice and the name of the person wearing the coat with a professional title, if any.

This also takes away the distraction of varied attire and is the easiest way to immediately identify professionalism. These coats should be replaced often, as the repeated cleanings take a toll on the fabric.

White is the only color to consider. White says clinical. The embroidery can reflect the color of the practice with thread color choice and even adding the practice logo. The lab coats should continue the branding of the practice. The doctor's coat should be long, with all others shorter. This is one more way to set the doctor apart and also improve the professional image of the office. Everyone should have at least 2 coats. If soiled, another is immediately available for change.

"Failure is not to be feared. It is from failure that most growth comes; provided that one can recognize it, admit it, learn from it, rise about it, and try again."

Dee Hock, Visa

The Room of the Practice

The procedure room helps to complete not only the concierge image of the practice but it also helps to put the patient at ease. When I want to turn a plain room into a spa room, I barter the transition. Remember, I've had zero budget to soften the clinical room and create a spa-like atmosphere. Most designers are concerned with their own appearance, and are often willing to work out a trade for fillers and toxins.

The room should be relaxing and calming. Even though we are comfortable with the process, the process frightens new and returning patients. A waterfall in the room goes a long way to create calm, as well as masking the other noises in the office. Soft background music should also be playing to create a calming effect.

No one looks good in bad light. Drape beautiful sheer fabric on bamboo poles just under the light. Do not overlook the importance of accent rugs. They help to absorb sound and add to the ambiance. Select furniture to display products. A beautiful armoire helps to create a homey feel. The power of fragrance also calms. There are many options for relaxing fragrances, so choose one that works with the size of your room.

Pick a color for the practice and carry out the theme and brand of your practice. Remember to include everything from the embroidery on the lab coats, the towels, the colors of the room, the business cards, the brochures as well as the promotional materials. Continue branding the practice at every opportunity so the patient knows your brand. Offer your signature spa treatment robe, slippers and towels for retail sale. People love branded products. They make Fabulous add-ons and Fabulous gifts especially during the holidays.

The treatment chair should be comfortable for the patient and adjustable for the injector. One important feature is for the chair to form a flat surface. If the patient turns pale and feels clammy, it is time to have them lay flat and the chair should do that for you.

Having ice packs in the room are important. A small refrigerator behind a beautiful folding screen not only looks Fabulous but it is practical, too. When the injector finishes with one area, placing an ice pack on the newly treated area will help to sooth and help with vascular constriction.

In the concierge practice, the patient always goes home with fresh ice packs. The ice pack should be in the color of the practice with the name of the practice as well as any logo associated with the practice. Do not forget to also have the phone number and website printed on the ice pack along with on all promotional materials.

It can be cool in a procedure room, so a soft blanket goes a long way in creating comfort for your patient. Under the blanket could be a heating pad to make the arrival of your patient warm. It is the unexpected, thoughtful touch that creates concierge service and ultimately multiple referrals from patients.

Another approach to comforting them, aside from a blanket, is to offer a large, thick and lush towel. The towel can be embroidered with positive statements randomly on the towel to further create the spa-like experience. I like words like peace, happiness, joy, beauty, kindness, and fabulous sprinkled on the towel. Do not forget to have the practice name and logo in the colors of the practice also embroidered to continue the branding initiatives.

The room of the practice should also include a release for all products used and a consent to treat. These basic forms are available from all manufacturers and can be expanded to fit your practice. Once again, branding is important. The font and colors should be consistent. The practice logo helps to brand the release and thus keeping consistency.

A general information questionnaire is also important. Aside from the standard information consisting of name, address, etc., it is important to ask about previous treatments, whether fillers or facials, skin care regime or skin condition, allergies and current needs. This gives you additional permission to discuss add-ons to fillers and toxins and skincare...add-ons like facials, chemical peels, microdermabrasion, laser and radio frequency along with a skin care regime can address their needs and concerns.

For all new patients, always take them on a tour of your facility. It is a Fabulous way to introduce all of your services as you tour the building. Giving them brochures full of services with any special promotions featuring some of the slower moving treatments is important, too. You may consider offering everyone a gift certificate for a service or discount to give to a friend. It is a great way to obtain referrals. If they like what they saw and/or heard, they will happily share with a friend.

"A customer is the most important person ever in this office – in person or by mail."

Leon Leonwood Bean, L.L. Bean

Employees of the Practice

Catch your employees doing something correctly.

Catch your employees doing something above and beyond.

Catch your employees giving concierge service where "The answer to the question is yes, now what is the question?"

When you catch your employees doing something Fabulous, reward them with reward points. These reward points can be redeemed for services, gift certificates to local restaurants, personal time off, money, etc. As I mentioned earlier, we do a lot of pre-selling. I have trained appropriate people in the practice to call clients that have had fillers in the past but that we have not seen for 3, 6, 9, or even 12 months. I do not allow phone calls without a call to action. Invite the patient back in for a complimentary face check to see if they could benefit from additional filler and give them a call to action to purchase any product that might be needed at a reduced price by paying for it over the phone with a credit card.

The product can be used over the next 12 months and the patient can request a refund at any time. I reward the employee making the phone calls and making the pre-purchases with $10 cash for every syringe pre-sold.

The employee comes to me and I count out $10 bills equaling the number of syringes appearing on the charge card receipt. This has proven to be successful in creating cash flow and monies into the office prior to ordering product. The employees like it so much, sometimes if they have 15 minutes remaining in their lunch hour, they will ask for a list of people to call.

If the employee needs new shoes and wants to pay cash all they need to do is sit and make a few calls. If the employee needs new shoes, all they need to buy those shoes is to sit down and make some phone calls. Putting extra money in their hands makes them happy. Another way to keep and retain happy employees is to offer them incentives on package services. Feature series of three facials along with microdermabrasion or any combination of services with a different service included. This gives the client the ability to try other services you offer. Reward the employee who sells this series or package of services with a gift certificate to a local restaurant. This is a win-win situation. The employee no longer has to cook after work and you both can put more money in the bank. A happy employee is a faithful employee.

After any treatments, have you employee suggest skin care to ensure the best results. We all know if the correct skin care is used after any service, the patient will see better results. Reward the employee with a commission and/or reward for the add-on and for a Fabulous job done.

At staff meetings, have a grab bag for all employees recognized for Fabulous service...an employee could be nominated by another employee or a patient could have complimented them for going above and beyond...an employee that gave concierge service where the answer to the question is yes, now what is the question.

The employee reaches into a bag containing $500. Each envelope has one bill in it. It could be a $1, $5, $10, $20, or $50 and be sure to tell everyone attending the amounts in the envelopes. One day someone at the meeting will pull out a $50 for all to see. Do this at every staff meeting to build excitement and anticipation to see which employee will pull out how much money? At the annual holiday party be sure to recognize outstanding performance. It could be best retail sales for the year, most requested employee for services, best receptionist, and again, limited only by your imagination.

Before all employee meetings, ask everyone to bring suggestions to improve business.

Reward all employees that brought ideas that you plan to implement.

At the meeting have an employee present an article they found and pre-researched that could impact business.

Set retail and service goals.

Post a chart in the break room and have employees update their chart daily to keep them aware of their progress. This gives you a Fabulous way to know who needs additional training and who need praise and encouragement. This is Fabulous information for the meetings, as well.

Each month at the meeting, have grab bags for everyone that met their goals. The bag could have products, gift certificates, treatments or whatever you imagination allows.

Be sure and keep products for purchase out and visable for patients to try. Remember if the patient cannot steal it, they will not buy it. Remember 99.9% will not ask for something that is locked away. Everything should be available to touch, smell and sample.

Have a logo bag with tissue for all purchases. If that is not in your budget yet, go to a party store and purchase colorful bags and tissue. Add a label that has the practice name hand-written in gold ink. (Remember, gold implies status.)

Be sure your retail center is Fabulous at all times. Remember retail never calls in sick. Call other practices within 10 miles and see what retail products they sell and make sure you sell something different. Smaller companies are eager for your business and will give more incentives than the larger companies that are in most offices.

Patients are overwhelmed with more than 3 product choices. Keep it simple and concise. Too many choices confuse even the savviest shopper. At every staff meeting, include a retail segment. Give everyone a different product and 5 minutes to prepare a brief presentation on the value of the product. Offer a reward to the most outstanding presentation with the product they presented. Be sure and send home a prescription with every patient that tells them what skincare they need, but did not purchase.

Use shelf talkers in front of featured products. Most home goods have place card holders. Write the product benefits in gold ink. It is a silent salesperson that you can change at any time. When showing product, always say the magic words, "This is what I recommend."

People want to know what you use, like and what you recommend for them. Have a special promotion to exchange your patient's products. Have your patient bring in products they are currently using and exchange them for products you have for purchase. The patient receives 25% off the purchase price of your products and you keep the old product. You have just switched the patient to your line and you did not have to spend money on advertising.

Have patients keep their receipts and for every $1000 or $1500 they have spent in your practice on retail, and they will receive a gift certificate. You can keep track of you patient's purchases and when they are close, you could send them a handwritten note that they are nearing a gift certificate. Offer a VIP membership or Concierge membership for purchase. Whatever you deem the value is of $250, $500, or $1000. The patient receives 10% off the purchase of all products and services.

They also receive a service of choice at no cost each year. They are invited to an annual exclusive champagne party to introduce new products and services. You can take it as far as you like. If you charge on the higher end, you could also include a same-day service guarantee with extended time for all appointments. Once again depending on the dollars charged, your imagination can be your guide.

An employee advisory board is a Fabulous way to recognize key employees and get valuable information. Meet once a month for lunch and review the business and ask for suggestions on ways to improve. Be sure and pay for lunch and thank everyone for participating. An advisory board from your most valuable patients is another way to review ideas of adding services and products and get the patients' ideas.

This board could meet quarterly for lunch and do not forget to pay for lunch. An advisory board for the practice from within the community is also a valuable tool to garner ideas. Local bankers, accountants, public relations, vendors, marketing, etc. can meet once a month for lunch and ideas. Do not forget to pay for lunch. All of the boards could meet annually for recognition and to help create the cohesive team to build business.

"Wealth, like happiness, is never attained when sought after directly. It comes as a by-product of providing a useful service."

HENRY FORD, FORD MOTOR COMPANY

Marketing the Practice

Work with your local realtors. Provide information about your practice along with a gift certificate for a service to be included with their 'welcome to the neighborhood' basket. When a certain number are redeemed, the realtor gets to also enjoy a complimentary service.

Pick a few of your best patients and give them 2 gift certificates for free services in the practice. Ask them to give the gift certificates to people much like themselves that you have not already met. Be sure to let your best patients know that you appreciate their support and when the gift certificates are redeemed, offer your best patients a complimentary service, as well.

When you do events at your practice, find a charity that you believe in and promote the event as a fundraiser for the charity. Alert the local media and you may find your practice featured in the paper for a no-cost advertisement.

Most local papers have a luminary section. When you see a local featured, clip the ad and have it laminated. Mail the laminated ad with a gift certificate to the person with praise for their Fabulous contribution of time, service and/or money to a worthy cause.

Most cities have local celebrities. Invite them into the practice for a complimentary service. While in your practice, talk to them about doing a video of services and ask for an endorsement. You may choose to do fillers and toxins in return for one before and after video. The second video could be laser, with a third about radio frequency. All of the videos should be used on your website and sent for a targeted advertising campaign with a send out email service that costs very little. Videos can be put on multimedia sources for no-cost advertising. You could ask for a testimonial from the local celebrity to put on you website, as well.

A business plan is one of the most important tools in you marketing plan. How do you know where you are going without a business plan? How many fillers you are selling for first quarter…how much toxin in second quarter…what will retail sales produce in third quarter…how will the VIP program produce revenue in fourth quarter and on and on. This is your road map to know where your business is headed. In addition to your business and marketing plan, list your strengths, your weaknesses, your opportunities and your threats and review each quarter to see how the dynamics change.

Consider adding an easy-to-open credit plan to overcome objections when doing consultations. Many people do not have the disposable income to do large services on a whim, but given the opportunity to make payment, (sometimes without interest) can make the difference between yes and no.

Most of the programs like Care Credit can be opened in minutes while the patient is in the office so the service can be performed the same day as the consultation.

Just offering the service during a consultation when they say they cannot afford to do services the same day, can cause the patient to disclose that they really can afford to do the service, and in fact, they had already planned to write a check or pay with cash they have been saving for this occasion. You can also use this service in promotions especially when the companies offer the option of no interest for 12 months.

Your employees should be some of your best marketers. Everyone in the practice should experience all services in the practice to be able to talk about them to others not only in the office but outside, as well.

When hiring someone new, present a plan of action that allows the new employee to experience all services over a controlled amount of time and present it as a benefit of employment. Employees that have been with you for an extended amount of time are even more valuable. They should revisit all of the services as part of their ever-growing benefit package.

It is much more effective to keep an employee than hiring a new employee. Protect your investment and keep your Fabulous and well-trained employees. We all have the weakest link and should always be open to replacing the weakest link when that perfect opportunity arises.

A simple marketing strategy in the office is having a well-trained staff. All employees should promote each other. When the first contact with the patient is about to turn over the patient to another employee in the practice, they are building up the employee that the patient is about to meet. Talk about the person's credentials, training, expertise, kindness, abilities and how the patient is going to enjoy working with the employee and how Fabulous the experience is going to be.

Each time someone is turned over to another employee, the process continues. The best marketing in the office can be from the employees. Also, every employee should wear a name tag with a conversation starter. Something as simple as, "I grew up in Boston" or "I am a vegetarian" can start a conversation and make the patient feel more comfortable.

Another simple marketing tool in the office with a new patient is a 'welcome to the practice' packet. It could include a welcome letter, biography of the injector, a patient friendly CD, overview of services and information about events, any current and/or future specials and a 'meet the team' listing.

Have each team member write in their biography not only the pertinent information, but also include what their favorite service is within the practice. Another convenience for new patients could include a page of before and after photos so the new patient can choose exactly what they want. A quick, simple and straight to-the-point approach that makes it easy for a new patient that is already confused and concerned.

We all know the importance of a Fabulous website and many take pride in their website. Most websites have Contact Us page. This is a golden opportunity to develop new patients. They are writing with a reason and intent. All questions or comments – all correspondence should be answered within 48 hours, tops. It really should be less than 24 hours.

In office marketing can be as simple as displaying the injectors credentials. Do not hide diplomas in the injector's office where most people will never see. Display them proudly in the consultation room, the injection room or somewhere the patients can see, read and become more confident in their choice of your practice. By the time the patient meets the injector, there should be no questions of ability. The more credentials displayed, the more fears are alleviated.

Before and after books with pictures of actual patients is another valuable in-office marketing tool. These picture books should be professional and appealing with the name of the product used and number of syringes used to achieve the results.

This is another tool to educate the patient on the need for quantity of product to achieve transformational results. The picture books should also include the practice story and biographies of injectors. With each picture, you could include a patient tip that the patient gave you when they signed their photo release. These books can be completed locally or ordered easily online at companies like Kodak. Remember no magazines - only have before and after books along with brochures from manufactures and the practice.

I believe the most important take-home message for marketing is to create some kind of loyalty program. It is so much easier to retain a patient than it is to bring a new one into the practice. It is also less expensive to retain a patient than spend money, time and effort to attract a new patient.

When a patient is leaving, it is effective to take them to an area that is not only private, quiet and calm, but also informative. Display cards with before and after pictures of all of the areas you do within your practice. This gives you the ability to hand the patient a card with the practice information once again and remind them that this was an area we discussed in the consultation but did not complete today. It gives the patient a friendly reminder of what can be accomplished.

"Do something. Either lead, follow or get out of the way."

Ted Turner, CNN

The Worksheet of the Practice

Your Goals

What is your vision of Fabulous success? Imagine you have launched your Fabulous campaign and it is a Fabulous success. What does that success look like?

What will be your Fabulous call to action? What action do you want your patients to take?

Your Audience

Understand who your Fabulous patient is so you can make an offer that appeals.

What do your Fabulous patients need?

What is the demographic? How old, income, gender?

Your Practice

What service or product do you provide that makes a difference in a patient's life?

Why does your patient need you? What makes your practice Fabulous?

The Fabulous Offer

Write the offer. Why do they come to your practice? What will make them come again?

Close the Fabulous offer with a call to action. What do you want the patient to do?

Write a Fabulous message to encourage your patient to share your offer.

Write you subject line. 4-10 words sums up your Fabulous offer.

Write your headline. Keep it simple. Patients should know what you are offering from your headline.

Day One

Send your offer. Post your Fabulous offer on social networks and email the invitation.

Day Two

Post your campaign with follow up information. Keep the excitement going by posting engaging content. Elaborate on you offer.

Day Three

See how you are doing. Take a look and see what is working and where you can improve your Fabulous offer.

Day Four

Start a Fabulous conversation with your patients. Ask your patients what they think. Ask a question about your campaign… maybe a fill-in-the-blank question.

Day Five

Let your patients know this Fabulous offer cannot be missed. Send the offer again and change the subject line. Limited appointments or limited quantities can be helpful. Repeat your Fabulous offer.

Day Six

Your Fabulous Event.

Day Seven

Send a Fabulous Thank You for taking action on your offer.

"The most important decision is how to position your product."

DAVID OGILVY, OGILVY & MATHER

Revenue of the Practice

Do what no one else is doing. Set your practice apart. Do what the other practices are not doing. If you want the success of the other practices and nothing more, then you can imitate what they are doing. If you want more, do more!

Have your concierge answer the phone by transferring the call to their cell phone. No other practice does that I bet, so do what they are *not* doing. The unexpected answer will capture a patient because they are accustomed to an answering service, not an employee.

Also, do some of the ideas described below to increase revenue and do what the other practices are not doing…until they read this book, that is. These techniques work. I have proven them over and over throughout the US, at many practices, while doing practice building for the physician, as well as other businesses.

I continue to do practice and business building as a passion and I can help your practice. Call me at 772-453-4137 and invite me to your practice. I will do role-play with your employees. I will teach them how to turn a phone call into a consultation. I will teach them how to turn a consultation into a same day service, not an estimate. Learning how to make pre-sale phone calls will increase employee loyalty by increasing their income and it will also increase revenue for the practice. Putting together the perfect event can also give the practice an immediate cash flow infusion. Learning how to negotiate the best deals from the suppliers can additionally save revenue for the practice.

A VIP program is a valuable asset for the practice. I think the VIP should be simple. Too many practices make their VIP program complicated with points and purchase requirements and so many rules that no one can understand the program, must less participate. I think (3) is a maximum for programs.

What I recommend is:

VIP Silver - $500 – The patient receives toxins and fillers at event pricing (usually $200 less than regular price) at any time. The patient does not have to come to an event or pre-purchase any toxins and/or fillers. The patient also receives one free service that requires multiple services to receive maximum results. The service could be a facial, micro-dermabrasion, chemical peel, RF, IPL, light laser or one area laser hair removal. Whatever services you want to promote that requires multiple visits for maximum results, is ideal for your Silver VIP.

The VIP Silver basically costs you nothing and helps to assure your patients are loyal to your practice. I use the VIP Silver for gifts for drawing at events. I also use the VIP Silver to bring unknown patients into the practice. Provide the VIP Silver membership, which costs you nothing, to a local realtor to include in their welcome-to-the-neighborhood welcome package or to upscale apartment complexes for the same purpose.

The most successful way has been to provide it to the local gym. Everyone that purchases a membership receives a VIP Silver membership. Gyms attract people that are vane. Most members are trying to lose weight and/or look better. This is the patient you are looking for. Any business that has a vane customer or is upscale, is a possibility.

Another successful use was with country clubs, as a value-added piece for members…value added for the business to their customers that costs you nothing and brings in patients you do not currently serve. Check with your accountant, you may be able to claim a donation deduction especially if you provide to a nonprofit to raise funds. The nonprofit sells them and keeps the money and you receive the benefits. This membership can also be used for corporate gifts. It is ideal for the executive that does not know what to give his administrative assistant and/or secretary.

The VIP Gold - $1500 - is the most popular. For a purchase price of $1500, the patient has everything in the VIP Silver plus toxins for 12 months. The patient can come in as often as they like and pay nothing for toxins. The toxin patient is your least faithful patient. The toxin patient is constantly looking for the next dollar off a unit of toxin and will travel for the savings. Having the patient come in more often, say every month, for tweaking increases revenue. Every time the patient comes in they are required to have a consultation. With a consultation, more services will be needed.

The injector controls the number of units administered so you will never use more than the cost of the toxin and have more opportunity to sell the patient additional services and products while keeping them faithful to the practice. This is the most popular corporate gift and continues to be the most popular of the VIP memberships.

The VIP Platinum - $2000 – includes all of the VIP Silver and VIP Gold, plus skincare for a year. The patient receives an eye crème, moisturizer, and a cleanser every quarter. The patient has to come in to receive the products, so never mail the products. Every time the patients come in for products, they need a consultation to evaluate the skin again and most need additional products. Maybe a night crème, serum, and/or a sunscreen, etc. will be needed. This is the ultimate corporate gift.

These VIP memberships can be sold when someone comes in for toxins. The cost for treatment at the visit could be $400 but with the purchase of a VIP Gold or Platinum, there would be no cost for the treatment for the rest of the year. Even with the VIP Silver, the patient pays event prices rather than full price.

All of the VIP memberships can be pre-sold over the phone. Call and remind the patient it is time for their toxins and sell over the phone the VIP membership and reward the employee for the pre-sale. You can either reward the employee for cash or points. Points can be redeemed for whatever you decide. Points for time off with pay, points for services, points for products, and points for cash are all popular. It is limited only by your imagination. Every employee should have an incentive, whether it is commission in money or points to redeem for their choice. Even if the employee is on a salary, a commission structure to increase sales is a must. If you do not have one in place for every employee, including the front desk, injector, nurse, office staff, cleaning staff...yes, every member of your staff... put one into place today! Not tomorrow, not next week, not next quarter... TODAY... and watch your revenue increase.

If you are not a member of your local Chamber of Commerce, join. Go to every mixer the Chamber hosts. Monthly breakfast meetings can be a Fabulous way to meet new patients, as well as new businesses to partner with and have events with to increase business for both.

The business after hours is another way to mingle and meet new people and share your business. Every networking event is worth attending at least three times to see if the mixer is worth your time. Also consider hosting the business after hours for the Chamber. You can create your own networking mixer and host at your office. Martini Monday Mixers can be Fabulous and even better in your office. The movers and shakers learn about your practice and spread the word, while some become patients.

Using toxins as your lost leader eliminates the need to advertise. I do not believe in paid advertising. Events, open houses, VIP memberships, business after hours, constant contact, and social media can get your information out to the masses. The toxins become the draw. The toxin patient is the least faithful patient so use toxins as a hook to get them in the practice. Everyone coming in for low cost toxin must have a consultation because I am sure they need more than toxin. Even the young ones need lip augmentation and/or malar enhancement, so they don't have to use so much contour to create Fabulous cheek bones.

A Fabulous way to increase revenue is to rent a weekend kiosk at the mall and the doctor or one of the injectors is available for toxins and filler. Have a Fabulous person dressed to perfection walk around and hand out Fashion Fabulous Awards. She sees someone with Fabulous shoes and gives them an award for Fabulous hair, etc. On the other side of the Fashion Fabulous Award business card is the information about the practice and the event price and immediate availability with location.

You meet new people and gather more emails, names, addresses and phone numbers to add to your constant contact. Do not forget to write a hand-written, hand-addressed thank you note. You increase revenue and your contact list at the same time and it is only two days a week and can be rotated among the injectors.

Products can also be sold to add more to the total at the end of the day. Partner with some of the businesses surrounding your kiosk and with every so many people they send you, they receive free toxin. They can book all week for you and you arrive to a full book of injections. Still have the Fashion Fabulous Awards handed out as you always have time to add more patients.

An old fashion fan is a Fabulous promotional piece that the patient will keep. Fans were once used at funerals and weddings only but now they are Fabulous promotional pieces. I like to put the practice information on one side. Include the name, injector, address, phone, email, and website. The back side of the fan has the menu of services. Fans are kept and rarely throw out. One never knows when one might need a Fabulous Fan. The only place I purchase promotional fans is from Spa Stix. (www.spastix.com 855-292-7909) They also have the best quality and prices for waxing stix, medical stix, and eco stix. Spa Stix is a Fabulous company that manufactures the products and are not a middle man. If it is a wooden stix, they manufacture it at the best price available with 5 warehouse locations across the country for immediate delivery. Spa Stix is even able to print the name of your practice on any wooden product, like the fan handle. They print in-house so you get Fabulous turnaround time. It is days, not weeks.

Everyone in the office should have filler and toxin in their face. The manufacturers will provide product for staff use. Having fillers in their face helps to alleviate concerns of the patient in the consultation and increase revenue. Have one employee with 5 syringes, one with 10 syringes, one with 15 syringes and use them in the consultation when someone says that they could never do the 5, 10, or 15 syringes your concierge suggests in the consultation. Bring the person in with the appropriate number of syringes and show the patient that it takes volume replacement and this is just their beginner's kit. Most manufactures will provide the product if they understand what you want to accomplish. Toxin companies always want the staff smooth and will provide product for staff use. Staff likes the fact they are getting products at no cost and it is a Fabulous employee benefit that you can use as incentives for sales.

Never put a want ad in the paper. Always see the person in action and recruit. If you want a concierge, go to a cosmetic counter at an upscale department store and purchase a product like an eye crème or cleanser. If the person tries to sell additional products, wraps it in tissue, and brings your package around the counter to you, hand them a business card. Tell them that you are looking for someone much like them. If they have a brother, sister, friend much like themselves, have them call you. What you want is for them to call and most of the time they will call and say they want to talk about the position. An ad brings people in that do not have jobs and expect an interview and will be on their best behavior.

When you see them in action and they do not know you are interviewing them, you will know how they will perform when they work in your practice. Where you find an employee is only limited to your imagination. You can find a Fabulous employee that is currently a waiter, a deli worker, at a dress shop...you get the idea. If you want an additional aesthetician, go have a facial. If you want an additional massage therapist, go have a massage. Only interview when they do not know you are interviewing. This not only saves revenue for the practice, it also produces the best employees.

Packaging services and products increases revenue and increases results. Combining treatments such as laser and PRP, give measurably better results, better healing, better skin texture, and increased revenue and that is a plus.

Combining RF and PRP also gives dramatically better results and creates a happier patient that will refer and return. Microdermabrasion before a chemical peel will give more visual result and add skincare and you know you will have results that are remarkable. When you add skincare in the patients "to go" bag after treatment, you increase revenue as well as results. Be sure to combine skincare with the packages whether facials, chemical peels, micro-dermabrasion, and the more aggressive treatments, as well.

Packing skincare such as cleanser, moisturizer, and eye crème can be a simple package for everyone. This simple package can be pre-packaged for an easy and immediate sale. Package this simple package in oily, normal, dry, and troubled. More elaborate packages should also be available for greater revenue.

Gift with purchase is another way to close the sale. Most manufacturers will provide products for the gift to help increase sales of the skincare line they represent. I also do not believe in sampling, in general. If someone asks for a sample, my response is "no". I inform the patient that I have the product in a retail size with a full money-back refund after they have used all of the contents. I also use this when someone returns a skincare product after a short time, like 1 week. I tell the patient that they have to use the product until the container is empty, as they will not know for sure how well the product works until they use the product for at least 30 days.

I have found with this "bottom of the bottle" guarantee that it has virtually eliminated returns. When a patient uses the entire product, they find that they actually like the product and will purchase again. Combining products with toxin and fillers is another way to increase revenue. Having the patient take arnica prior to toxin and fillers can be beneficial, as well as lucrative. Putting vitamin K crème on the toxin and filler injection sites is beneficial and lucrative also. Every service has add-ons to increase positive results and increase positive revenue.

Supplements also increase revenue and results. Taking care of the inside in addition to the outside gives Fabulous results. Taking care of the inside is important as the patient ages and hormone replacement goes hand in hand. Hormone replace is simple and a Fabulous way to increase revenue. Hormone replacement brings additional patients and additional opportunities to sell toxins and filler. After all, everyone coming in for a consultation for hormone replacement is not complete until addressing the need for toxins and fillers. Hormone replacement is very popular and easy with the male patient. Hormone replacement therapy is an easy way to bring more male patients to your practice who are at the age of need for hormone replacement and need toxins and fillers. This patient is a lifetime patient as the hormone replacement only increases with age.

Blunt tip cannulas will change your filler practice in a Fabulous way. Using blunt tip cannulas, you can offer services with less discomfort, even a lip augmentation can be completed without the need for dental blocks or even topical numbing. The patient that comes in and has a needle phobia is calmed and more comfortable. The patient coming in and wants treatment today and has an occasion 3 days away, you can now consider doing the treatment with less concern of edema and/or bruising.

I am not a believer in expensive paid advertising. I believe you can use your toxins as your loss leader to attract new and returning patients. Fillers are your profit center, especially premier products like Artefill, the only FDA approved permanent filler on the market. I have a face full of Artefill for my liquid facelift. Toxins should be a breakeven or at least not your profit center. Fillers are your profit center. There is no service you can perform that produces the revenue of fillers.

My experience with fillers, especially those that everyone in town does not have, can produce $10,000 an hour. No procedure can produce that revenue and profit. You may charge $25,000 for a facelift but the pre and post time, the hand-holding, the calls, the staff and on and on diminishes revenue tremendously. Toys are the biggest waste of time and potential revenue in the office. Lasers, IPL, RF, and all the other toys the rep at the window wants to show you cannot produce the revenue and profits that fillers can produce. The time it takes for the procedure cannot produce the revenue of fillers. The cost of the equipment and upkeep for the maintenance contract will not produce the revenue of fillers. Once surgeons realize fillers are their profit center, many chose to put the scalpel down and pick up the syringe and make more money…quicker, easier, with less risk, and have more fun with immediate gratification.

Private Label Skincare with the physicians name on the product can increase revenue and give control back to the practice that the physicians want. Putting the physicians name on a product immediately lends credibility to the product. Private Label Skincare produces more profit than the name brands that many within walking distance from your practice currently carry.

Private Label Skincare should be medical grade and available only in the physician's office because of the ingredients. Every time a patient comes in for product replacement, a consultation should be done, as I am sure they need additional products like toxins, fillers and/or procedures. The Private Label Skincare is the skincare that is part of the VIP Platinum and the skincare that is packaged with services. Your private label skincare is compounded with at least one proprietary ingredient. This proprietary ingredient, available at the compounding manufacturer, makes your skincare available through you practice alone, throughout the world.

Set yourself apart. Do what no one else is doing. If you want what others have, do what they are doing. If you want more, do something different. When the concierge is doing the consultation, be sure to include a skin analysis and make recommendation for skincare. Give the information to the doctor and have the doctor write a prescription for the skincare before leaving after completion of services. The concierge has all of the products wrapped in tissue and in a bag baring the name and information of the practice and is waiting at the checkout point and is added to the total for services. The assumptive close works, use it. Assume the patient wants the products…after all why would they not??? Make the patient tell you they do not want the products and then question why. The skincare regime prescribed by the doctor is what the patient needs just like any other prescription and will make their skin Fabulous. The patient would not want to be anything less than Fabulous, would they???

Most practices want testimonials for their website, framed in the consultation room, compiled in a book for the patient to read while they are alone for that brief time or anywhere you might deem appropriate. Offer patients with Fabulous outcomes an incentive for allowing you to use their before and after photos with a written testimonial including their name. One appropriate gift would be the VIP Silver membership that cost you nothing and has a value of $500 to the patient. The VIP testimonial member could be part of your patient advisory committee that meets monthly and/or quarterly to give the practice a perspective from the patient point of view. Even the patients that did not have the best visual results or the patient just does not want their pictures used is still Fabulous for written testimonials.

Barcodes have become so common and beneficial in marketing now that our smart phones are able to read them and go to the website, why not use them in your practice. Have magnets for the refrigerator made with practice information and a barcode. When the patient reads the barcode with their smart phone it goes to a daily, weekly, or monthly special for your practice. A wonderful way to keep patients loyal to your practice and increase revenue at the same time and it says your practice is on the cutting edge of technology.

Every practice experiences cancellations and they can destroy a profitable day and turn it into a day not worth opening. Have an email list that you can immediately send out a standardized email stating that if someone can take a specific appointment time, the patient receives a discount. It can also be on Facebook and Twitter. It needs to be enough of a call to action to make it worth the patient's time to change their plans and come spend money with your practice. I believe somewhere between 25%

and 50% is necessary for immediate action on the patient's part. After all, a service with a reduced profit is better than no service and no profit and it fills the day again, as well as gets the patient in the habit of coming to the office more often.

Pre-Sales

Pre-sales can create substantial cash flow to purchase product. I taught the people in the practice to get on the phone and sell, rather than be on the computer or read a magazine. I would do the pre-sale training while they listened and then had them role play.

Next, I would give them a couple of names that I did not care if they burned through without success. Then, it is important for more role play to overcome objections.

The key to pre-sales is to compile a list of patients that have had fillers but not within the last 3 months. The most successful has been the 3-12 month time range, since the last treatments.

I would call them, stating it was time to come in for a face check to see how they are doing with the project of their face. I offer them the opportunity to pre-purchase at the time of the phone call at a special price.

They give me the credit card number and I charge the patient for as many as they want to pre-purchase. I reward the people in the office that call, $10 cash for each syringe they sell. The person brings me a receipt for 5 syringes paid for with a charge receipt and I count out (5) $10 bills. This has been a very successful program.

For someone on an hourly salary, this can make a substantial difference. We have sold hundreds of syringes on pre-purchase. I tell the patient that if they change their minds, I will refund their purchase immediately. The patient has 12 months to use the product and also saves money.

If the patient says they are not interested, I say I will mark their chart that they will be at the higher price when they come in for their visit. This gives a reason for the call to schedule them to come in and also a call to action to purchase today. I also use this for events, as well.

"In order to be irreplaceable one must always be different."

COCO CHANEL

Event Synopsis

Open houses for many are a mixed bag. Sometimes they are Fabulous, but most likely not, since they are the people that are already part of the practice.

Events held outside the practice to generate new patients for the practice, are most beneficial. Events outside the practice allow you to grow your email list to new and different people within the community.

I have had events at many different businesses – coffee shops, delis, dress shops, day spas, wine and cheese shops, etc. You can see the diversity. The deli was one of the most unusual and one of the most successful.

I go into a business and ask to speak with the owner. I say I would like to host an event for them in their business for their customers, friends, family, neighbors, etc. I will bring a doctor to do toxins and fillers at special event pricing.

All I need from them is their email list to add to ours in order to send out the invitation. The doctor will most likely say, "I do not do things like that; after all I am a doctor." My response is always, "It is time to get out of your own way!" If you expect different results doing what you have always done, we all know the definition.

"A thing of beauty is a joy forever:
Its loveliness increases; it will never
Pass into nothingness."

JOHN KEATS, ENDYMION

Business Card Trick

If you have a busy sidewalk and no one is noticing you...

If you are near the subway and no one is noticing you...

If you are not getting noticed and want to be noticed...

Print a two sided business card. One side has all your information. Practice name, address, phone number, website, email, etc.

The other side is a Fashion Award.

Stand on the busy sidewalk or near the subway and pass out fashion awards. Someone walks by with Fabulous shoes, a Fabulous handbag, a Fabulous outfit, you get the idea, say to them, "Your shoes are Fabulous...here is a Fashion Award." This can be used walking in the mall, at a networking meeting; anywhere you use your imagination.

This is a positive take on the famous Fashion Citation. We can always find fashionistas to give the cards to and it is a Fabulous way to get your information out without looking desperate like a flyer can, sometimes. I also along with my practice information will include Botox $8 a unit with this card. Once again I do not care if I make money on toxins. I want the new patient because they bring their filler business with them when they come for Botox. Botox is so often shopped for the best price and I find that the Botox customer alone is not the most loyal customer. Everyone coming in for a special price on Botox has to have a consultation and guess what, they need fillers and I plant the seed.

"A dream doesn't become reality through magic; it takes sweat, determination and hard work. "

COLIN POWELL

Testimonials

John Treadwell has been a true asset to our company and has an amazing ability to help a practice grow at a tremendous pace. Unlike many consultants, John offers a success blueprint that is simple and easily duplicated. I have had the pleasure of introducing John to practices across the country where he has opened their eyes to the possibilities of growth within their practice. If you are looking for proven strategies to increase your patient base and grow your bottom line, look no further! By following the steps in John's book you will experience a journey towards meeting and exceeding your financial goals, one patient at a time.

Joe Proctor | National Sales Director

<u>Suneva Medical | 5870 Pacific Center Blvd. | San Diego, CA 92121</u> Artefill® The Lasting Solution™

John is an amazing and unique resource for any practice committed to being the best they can be. He not only understands how to generate practice patient flow through unique events, but more importantly how to create a long-lasting relationship with those patients. John builds those relationships with un-matched service, an honest and upfront discussion of the patient's aesthetic goals and what is required to reach them, combined with the excellent aesthetic outcomes delivered by the practice. His approach creates not only long-term patient relationships but advocates for the practice – patients highly satisfied with not only their cosmetic outcome but with every aspect of their interactions. Through this book you will gain insight directly into John's approach and best practice – and learn the key to his patient centric model: "The answer is yes, now what is the patient's request?"

Doug Abel
Executive Vice President, Commercial Operations
Suneva Medical, Inc.
5870 Pacific Center Boulevard
San Diego, CA 92121
858.550.9999 Extension: 5496
dabel@sunevamedical.com
www.sunevamedical.com

Additional Quotes

King Gillette, Gillette Razors

"There is no other article for individual use so universally known or widely distributed. In my travels, I have found it in the most northern town in Norway and in the heart of the Sahara Desert."

"The greatest feature of the business is the almost endless chain of blade consumption, each razor paying tribute to the company as long as the user lives."

Ingvar Kamprad, IKEA

"Waste of resources is a mortal sin at IKEA."

"Only those who are asleep make no mistakes."

"IKEA is not completely perfect. It irritates me to death to hear it said that IKEA is the best company in the world. We are going the right way to becoming it, for sure, but we are not there yet."

Estee Lauder

"You get more bees with honey."

"When you stop talking, you've lost your customer. When you turn your back, you've lost her."

Henry Heinz, H.J. Heinz Company

"Heart power is less than horse power."

"A wide market awaits the manufacturer of food products who sets purity and quality above everything else in their preparation. "

"To do a common thing uncommonly well brings success."

Issy Sharp, Four Seasons Hotels

"If someone had told me 'Look, you're going to start today and spend the next five years wasting your time trying to get this thing start', I would have said I can't do that. But you never think about what it's going to take of you. Think: I've got it now."

"Whatever you do, don't ever use a crutch, and don't ever think of having an excuse for not having said, 'Yeah, I did my best.'"

S. Truett Cathy, Chick-fil-A

"People want to work with a person, not for a company."

"I realized I could do anything if I wanted it badly enough."

J.K. Rowling, Harry Potter

"It is our choices that show what we truly are, far more than our abilities."

"Destiny is a name often given in retrospect to choices that had dramatic consequences."

"Anything's possible if you've got enough nerve. I was determined to try. I was determined to try because, frankly, my life was such a mess at this point, what – what was the worst that could happen? Everyone turn me down? Big deal."

Robert Johnson, BET

"BET was a business opportunity waiting for someone to put it together."

"If there's something I can do and I feel it should be done, I just want to do it. I just don't want to leave it undone because I'll sit back and say, why didn't I do that? Why didn't I start that business?"

"Anything that has to do with money, I want to be in that business."

Howard Hughes, Hughes Aircraft

"I intend to be the greatest golfer in the world, the finest film producer in Hollywood, the greatest pilot in the world, and the richest man in the world."

"I certainly would not ask somebody else to fly a plane if I were afraid to do it myself."

"The trouble with my life is that I do not think I am cut out to sit behind a desk."

Gerry Schwartz, Onex

"The hardest lesson I've learned has been to not repeat the dumb mistakes I've made over the years, which are too numerous to list."

"I'm still a long distance from smart. But I'm also a long distance from dumb."

"There is no such thing as high returns without risk."

Dee Hock, Visa

"If you don't understand that you work for your mislabeled 'subordinates,' then you know nothing of leadership. You know only tyranny."

"Given the right circumstances, from no more than dreams, determination, and the liberty to try, quite ordinary people consistently do extraordinary things."

Calvin Klein

"I think fantasies are for the birds. If there's something I want, nothing stops me."

"You can't advertise for one group. Otherwise, you end up having a very small business!"

"Doing everything as well as possible meant survival."

Philip Knight, Nike

"Ultimately, we wanted Nike to be the world's best sports and fitness company. Once you say that, you have a focus."

"The trouble in America is not that we are making too many mistakes, but that we are making too few."

"Everybody wants a certain amount of stress. Most people have too much, but I didn't want too little, either."

Ralph Lauren, Polo Ralph Lauren

"The best thing you can do is go away from this saying, 'I can do this too,' because it's all possible and I'm living proof."

"I'm totally involved with all of my products. Everything I make is my message and for years my goal has been to make the things I love."

"Back then when I mentioned Polo most people would look at me funny and say 'You mean like Marco Polo?'"

William Wrigley Jr., Wrigley Chewing Gum

"Even in a little thing like a stick of gum, quality is important."

"Nothing great was ever achieved without enthusiasm."

Leon Leonwood Bean, L.L. Bean

"Above all, we wish to avoid having a dissatisfied customer."

"We consider our customers a part of our organization, and we want them to feel free to make any criticism they see fit in regard to our merchandise or service."

Henry Ford, Ford Motor Company

"A market is never saturated with a good product, but it is very quickly saturated with a bad one."

"Most people get ahead during the time that others waste."

Pierre Omidyar, eBay

"You should pursue your passion. If you're passionate about something and you work hard, then I think you will be successful."

"You have to really believe in what you're doing, be passionate enough about it so that you will put in the hours and hard work that it takes to actually succeed there, and then you'll be successful."

"I was raised with the notion that you can do pretty much do anything you want. I always kind of just went ahead and tried things."

George Lucas, Lucasfilm

"I'm extremely grateful that I discovered my passion. I love movies. I love to watch them, I love to make them."

"It's hard work making movies…if you don't really love it, then it ain't worth it."

"I got the licensing rights because I figured they wouldn't promote the film and if I got T-shirts and things out there with the name of the film on them it would help promote the movie."

Ted Turner, CNN

"Watch me. I'm like a bulldog that won't let go."

"You can never quit. Winners never quit, and quitters never win."

Bonus : David Ogilvy, Ogilvy & Mather

"The most important decision is how to position your product."

"The psychiatrists say that everybody should have a hobby. The hobby I recommend is advertising."

"Raise your sights! Blaze new trails!! Compete with the immortals!!!"

www.ingramcontent.com/pod-product-compliance
Lightning Source LLC
Chambersburg PA
CBHW041712200326
41519CB00001B/134

* 9 7 8 0 9 8 2 7 7 3 7 2 7 *